GET THE JOB AT GOOGLE

THE EASY GUIDES TO GREAT JOBS

Get the job at Google
Published by Olfina L.L.C.
www.olfina.com

Olfina L.L.C. is independent and not associated with any product, vendor or company mentioned in this book.

For information about permission to reproduce selections from this publication or for general inquiries, please contact us online at www.olfina.com.

Library of Congress CIP Data is available.

ABOUT THE AUTHORS

Ninfa Chavez: With 10 years experience as a professional recruiter for leading corporations and staffing agencies, Ninfa offers a fresh perspective for those on both sides of the interview process. Having placed hundreds of candidates, her expertise spans a range of industries including technology, pharmaceutical, banking, medical and allied health. Upon graduating Florida Southern with an honors degree in psychology, Ninfa believed professional recruitment was the most positive way she could apply her background in psychology.

Currently a professional recruiter for Miami Children's Hospital, Ninfa previously served in the role of Recruitment Manager for Norwegian Cruise Line where she managed, coached and developed a team of 17 field recruiters. Her recruitment background includes the corporate environments of Bank of America and Invivo (a subsidiary of Philips), and leading staffing agencies, Kforce and Smith Hanley Consulting Group. Passionate about recruiting, Ninfa volunteers her time to help job candidates prepare their resumes. In her down time, she plays the violin, surfs, paints and enjoys playing with her two little dogs, Keshi and Matisse.

Olivier Buigues: Throughout his career, Olivier has been interviewed by many multinationals across the globe. He worked in finance in London (UBS Asset Management) in consulting in Madrid (Frontier Management Consultants) and in hospitality in Club Med. He later specialized in marketing and worked his way up the hierarchy in Sony Europe, Sony Latin America and Sony America. After returning to Europe as Marketing Director at the headquarters of Philips in Amsterdam, Olivier opened a Telecommunication Business in France, his home country. He now regularly conducts interviews for his company. Olivier Buigues holds a B.A. in Economics from the ULB and a Master's degree in Management from ESCP-Europe.

TABLE OF CONTENTS

TABLE OF FIGURES

INTRODUCTION

Your Future – Is There An App For That?

Everybody has heard of the incredible perks offered by Google. The media regularly covers the Googleplex and its free organic food, massages, pools... But the truth is that working at Google means helping people connect, communicate, and access information which can change the world.

That's why getting a job at Google is much more than simply landing employment with a top company. It's a noble way of sharing your skills and talents with humankind.

Exaggeration? The founders of Google don't seem to think so. Take a look at the company's mission statement since day one:

Google's mission is to organize the world's information and make it universally accessible and useful.

Imagine working on code for a Google product – let's say Google Android – then seeing it embraced by hundreds of millions global users. Wow.

Now that you're feeling inspired, The question remains: How can you improve your chances at landing a job at Google?

This Is Where We Come In.

We've conducted extensive research and have assessed Google's recruitment process from the perspective of an executive recruiter. The information we've compiled is the most current available. As you know, the Internet is jammed with advice on how to get a job at Google with the vast majority focused on landing a software engineering position.

Rather than duplicate this advice, we've focused on ways you can navigate the Google selection process while providing interviewers the bio-data they look for in every job candidate.

The good news – everything we've uncovered indicates there are significantly more opportunities to land a Google job this year than in previous years.

A Brief History Of Google – A Bedtime Story For Geeks.

The year is 1995. Google's founders, Larry Page and Sergey Brin meet at Stanford University when Brin is assigned to give Page a tour of the campus. Sergey is 22, Larry is 21. A year later, the two computer science grad students begin working on what began as a dissertation theme: exploring the mathematical properties and link structure of the World Wide Web.

They collaborate on a search engine they name BackRub which determines the importance of individual web pages. BackRub operates on Stanford University's servers for over a year. In 1997, Larry and Sergey decide to change their search engine's name to Google. The new name is a play on the word *googol,* a mathematical term which represents the numeral 1 followed by 100 zeros.

In the summer of 1998, an investor cuts a check for $100,000 to a company that doesn't yet exist: Google, Inc. The young founders, still grad students, set up their office in a friend's garage. After incorporating their company in the state of California, they cash that investor's check and Google is officially born. *PC*

Magazine notices the new start-up "has an uncanny knack for returning extremely relevant results." The magazine lists Google among its Top 100 websites for 1998.

By February of 1999, Google outgrows its garage office and moves its eight employees, and Yoshka, the company dog, to offices in Palo Alto. The company continues to expand exponentially over the next three years. In 2001, Larry and Sergey recruit Eric Schmidt, a veteran Internet strategist from Novell, and install him in the role of Google's CEO. By March of 2004, Google moves its 800 employees to the now famous Googleplex in Mountain View, CA. By the close of the same year, Google's index of web pages has grown to 8-billion.

Enter the naysayers and critics. Financial reporters pounce on the fact Google's stock didn't do quite as well as the captains of Wall Street had predicted for 2004. The blame is laid on the founders. Larry and Sergey are accused of arrogance because they dared to do business differently. They dared to manage their company differently. They dared to create a corporate culture unlike any other.

The critics babble on for the next two years as Google continues to launch new, innovative products. Then, in 2006, Google buys YouTube for a whopping $1.65-billion and Google becomes the undisputed Masters of the Online Universe. This is the same year the Merriam-Webster Dictionary declares the word "google" as a new verb in American lexicon.

Fast forward to late 2010. Google's staff has grown to over 24,000 employees worldwide. Rumor has it the company is about to launch Google Circles -- a social media platform that will rival Facebook. According to the street talk, Google Circles will allow members to selectively share and filter content among social circles of their choosing.

Of course, the company refuses to confirm or deny any plans for a new social network. However, Google makes a number of intriguing announcements after the 2010 winter holidays.

Google 2011: Return Of The Visionaries.

January 20th

The tech world is abuzz with the news – Larry Page will take over as Google CEO; Eric Schmidt will be the Executive Chairman; and Sergey Brin's new title will be Co-Founder. Even more interesting, reports indicate Larry, Sergey and Eric had made this decision over the 2010 winter holidays. And it was Eric who announced the change on the Official Google Blog:

> *"Larry will now lead product development and technology strategy, his greatest strengths, and starting from April 4 he will take charge of our day-to-day operations as Google's Chief Executive Officer!... Larry, in my clear opinion, is ready to lead. Sergey has decided to devote his time and energy to strategic projects, in particular working on new products. His title will be Co-Founder. He's an innovator and entrepreneur to the core, and this role suits him perfectly."*

Google-watchers worldwide couldn't resist noting the obvious – if, after 10 years, Google's original founders are taking back the reins, something big is in the works. Five days later, another clue is released on the Google Blog.

January 25th

Alan Eustace, SVP of Engineering and Research, announces the of launch of a 2011 hiring spree:

> *"In 2010 we added more than 4,500 Googlers, primarily in engineering and sales: second only to 2007 when we added over 6,000 people to Google. I love Google because of our people. It's inspiring to be part of the team. And that's why I am excited about 2011—because it will be our biggest hiring year in company history. We're looking for top talent—across the board and around the globe—and we'll hire as many smart, creative people as we can to tackle some of the toughest challenges in computer science: like building a web-based operating system from scratch, instantly searching an index of more than 100 million gigabytes and even developing cars that drive themselves. There's something at Google for everyone— from geo, to enterprise, to video—with most of the work done in small teams, effectively working as start-ups. (The average number of software engineers on a project at Google is 3.5.) That's why the vast majority of our people stay with us, building their careers and taking on new challenges within the company."*

When Google says it's hiring, everyone listens. In fact, reports indicate Google received a record-setting 75,000 online applications within a week of the hiring spree announcement.

If you're feeling you've already missed your chance at landing a Google job, don't despair. When it comes to Google's methods for screening applicants, *"Many are called, few are chosen."* Google has a reputation for leaving a job opening vacant rather than risk hiring the wrong person.

Although the number of new hires isn't specified in the January 25th announcement, it's clear Google plans to hire significantly more than the 6,000 new employees hired in 2007. How many more? We think the number could go as high as 8,000. This includes a thousand or more new employees in Europe and beyond. Add to this, news reports reveal specific areas in which Google is seeking new talent, right now:

> *"Notice the language that Google uses in the recruiting documents: "software engineers, product managers, user-interface experts and others who have ideas for mobile apps." These new hires are going to be thought leaders and creative experts to take mobile applications (whether they run natively or in a mobile browser) to the next level and set new standards for the non-Google developers who increasingly are looking to Android as a platform of choice." ZDNet Blog, January 21, 2011*

> *"To try to catch up to Apple, deep-pocketed Google intends to grow its app community with the brute force technique of hiring engineers and product managers with mobile app expertise to build Android apps in-house…." Wired Magazine, February 1, 2011.*

> *"It looks like Google CFO Patrick Pichette wasn't kidding when he said that YouTube was one of Google's four areas of focus for 2011: the company plans to increase headcount at YouTube by 30% this year." SFGate, March 10, 2011.*

Let's Connect The Dots

- Google founder, Larry Page, is taking back the company reins in the role of CEO on April 4, 2011. He will focus on product development and technology strategy.

- Co-founder, Sergey Brin, will be devoting his time to new, strategic products.
- The company has embarked on the largest hiring spree in Google history.

We think it's clear. After a 10-year mega-growth cycle, the company is now focusing on what it does best— the creation and marketing of cool Google stuff.

In addition to adding engineering positions for Mobile Apps and Social Networking, the company needs to expand its Googler workforce in non-tech areas such as:

- Product Managers in a wide range of
- Advertising & Media
- Sales & Marketing
- Communications
- Partnership Development
- Finance & Credit
- Support & Administrative

> ## March 28, 2011, Google Hires "The Father Of Java."
>
> Dr. James Gosling announced on his blog he's taken a position at Google. Although Gosling does not reveal his job title, the press speculates the "Father of Java" will help grow Android. Gosling joins a stellar line-up of technology inventors on Google's staff:
>
> - Guido van Rossum, creator of the Python
> - Rob Pike, Limbo creator
> - Kenneth Thompson, creator of the B language and co-creator of Unix
> - Vinton Cerf, co-creator of TCP/IP
> - Mark Davis, the cofounder of Unicode

GOOGLE'S FLAT MANAGEMENT STRUCTURE

Google's *Flat Management Structure* fosters what's been characterized as a *Geek-Ruled Meritocracy* with a *Culture of Innovation*. When you understand the nuances of the flat organizational approach, you can more effectively *brand* yourself as the ideal Google job candidate.

Unlike hierarchical structures with multiple management levels, flat structures have very few layers of management. With the reduction of bureaucracy comes a much shorter chain. Much like a small entrepreneurial enterprise, employees are more committed to their projects and feel a greater investment in the company's success.

By flattening its management structure, Google …

- facilitates faster decisions, project approvals and greater flexibility.

- encourages the flow of ideas among all employees regardless of titles.

- gives employees more freedom to innovate and move forward with ideas.

- enhances project teamwork and collaboration between departments.

- greatly improves communication and information sharing.

- empowers employees to take charge, self manage and lead.

- creates a more democratic culture with a fully-engaged staff.

- is able to shorten the chain of approval and release new products faster.

Despite its size, Google can maintain its "small company," entrepreneurial synergy through organizing teams designed for hands-on development. Even new hires find they play a significant role on projects and are encouraged to hit the ground running. Add to this, Google shifts troops from project to project to keep ideas flowing. The result – a distinctively Google-y state of creative chaos and flux.

Those with a flexible work style, and those inspired by problem solving, thrive in such a culture. Those who require a structured hierarchy to perform will likely crash and burn. That's why Google's unique recruitment process is calibrated to screen out the latter work style.

"I think one of the hardest things to do is ensure that we are hiring people who possess the kind of traits that we're looking for in a Google-y employee. Google-y is defined as somebody who is fairly flexible, adaptable and not focusing on titles and hierarchy, and just gets stuff done." Stacy Savides Sullivan, Chief Culture Officer/HR Director, Google Inc.

THE GOOGLE
RECRUITMENT
PROCESS

Over the years, the Internet has been abuzz with interview stories, rumors, and myths, about Google's recruitment screening process. Add to this, Google HR/Recruitment has been perfecting its methods over time. However, the stages of the recruitment process remain unchanged and can take as long as two or more months to complete. The stages include:

- The Online Application and Résumé Submission
- The Voluntary Google Job Survey
- The Multiple Phone Screens
- The Day-Long On-Site Screen
- The Questions, Questions, Questions

WHAT GOOGLE WANTS IN A JOB CANDIDATE

It's no secret Google has always sought to hire super-smart, innovative people who possess the mental agility to turn ideas into awesome products. In its early years, the company earned a reputation for demanding a high GPA (a minimum 3.80 for engineers) while harboring a preference for ivy leaguers. Today, the Google Job Survey indicates a more holistic, behavioral approach is used to screen applicants.

Still, Google hires less than one-half of one percent of all applicants in any given year. Every applicant should be aware the screening process is focused on eliminating false positives. In fact, Google turns down applicants who would be top contenders at other tech companies. Why? Because a strong culture fit is crucial to the Google paradigm.

Bring your A-game

Your competition is fierce and Google's standards are stratospherically high. The title of this USA Today article says it all.

With 3,000 job applications a day, Google can be picky:

While grades matter, it takes more than an exceptional GPA. Here's what hiring managers are looking for:

- *Extracurricular activity junkies. "We don't want someone who just studied the whole time" at college, says Yolanda Mangolini, director of talent and outreach programs.*

- *Candidates who stretch beyond comfort. "What we're looking for primarily is someone who can do more than what they know," Harvey says. "Somebody who is flexible and can roll with the punches, not someone who can do just one job and puts his head down."*

- *Unique personalities. "Come prepared to discuss what makes you a unique candidate," Mangolini says. "We value distinct perspectives."*

THE COMPETITION – A RÉSUMÉ EVERY 25 SECONDS

In a 2010 survey of 10,000 American young professionals conducted by Universum, Google was ranked the number one "ideal employer."(Microsoft was ranked seventh.)

Universum conducted a separate student survey among 345 American universities encompassing 56,900 respondents. Google ranked number one among those students who chose *IT* or *Business* as their main field of study.

Considering these numbers, it should come as no surprise Google receives a résumé every 25 seconds, every day of the year. How does Google accomplish the herculean task of filtering 1-million-plus, top-tier applicants per year? You guessed it. They developed an algorithm.

THE STANDARDS – IS THERE AN ALGORITHM FOR THAT?

In 2007, Google surveyed hundreds of their current employees, and analyzed two-million data points, to develop a Google-y personality profile. With this bio-data, the search engine wizards developed an algorithm used to spot Google-worthy job applicants.

Google — in typical eccentric fashion — has created an automated way to search for talent among the more than 100,000 job applications it receives each month. It is starting to ask job applicants to fill out an elaborate online survey that explores their attitudes, behavior, personality and biographical details going back to high school.

The questions range from the age when applicants first got excited about computers to whether they have ever tutored or ever established a nonprofit organization. The answers are fed into a series of formulas created by Google's mathematicians that calculate a score — from zero to 100 — meant to predict how well a person will fit into its chaotic and competitive culture. New York Times, January 3, 2007

It's a brave new Google world, for sure. The good news? Although a high GPA is important, Google is less concerned with your GPA and more interested in your Google-y quotient.

YOUR GOOGLE DOSSIER

From the moment your submit your online application, résumé and job survey, Google begins to compile your bio-data. A tracking system coordinates data points collected by each phone interviewer and organizes it into a comprehensive dossier. All references you've provided will be contacted and their feedback is added to your dossier.

If you make it to the on-site interview, various interviewers will compile and enter more data. By the end of this process, your dossier becomes a comprehensive personal profile which the hiring committee uses in its decision process.

Naysayers have criticized Google's recruitment methods and are quick to point out it often results in the rejection of qualified candidates. However, when you understand the process is designed to identify specific behavioral traits, you can present yourself in a way which better fulfills their needs.

No, we're not talking about beating the system. We're talking about the need to highlight your true strengths and brand yourself as a solid contender for a Google job.

THE VOLUNTARY GOOGLE JOB SURVEY

When considering the best strategy we could use to prepare you for the Google recruitment process, we decided to start with *Google's Voluntary Job Survey* (which you complete online prior to your first phone interview). Why? Because this is the first point at which Google probes your behavioral traits.

Notice the word, *voluntary*? Yes, so did we. Of course, Google assures applicants they will not be penalized should they choose to skip the survey after submitting their résumé/CV. But let's use a bit of common sense – if you're applying to a company that collects, analyzes and essentially worships data, it's a good idea to offer bio-data about yourself. Especially when they ask politely.

Google's Job Survey is designed to identify the behavioral *soft skills* necessary to seamlessly fit into the company culture. To accomplish this, Google uses your responses to assess past behavior as an indicator of future behavior.

For example, if you were a team leader in elementary school, high school, and college, you're more likely to bring your leadership skills to the small teams at Google. These include listening to others, discussing ideas and methods, while focused on the end result. If you fell in love with computers at an early age, you'll continue to marvel and be intrigued by technology's infinite possibilities.

ANSWER the SURVEY QUESTIONS!

Without a doubt, completing this survey gives you an edge over those candidates who choose to skip it. In fact, by-passing the survey altogether may well reveal another behavioral trait: you're not willing to go the extra mile. And this attitude is simply not Google-y.

About the Survey...

The most intriguing thing about the *General Questions* section is it hasn't changed since first implemented. During our research we found an archived PDF of this document copyrighted in 2007. When we took a look at the 2011 version it was exactly the same. What does this tell us? Google's algorithm is accurately identifying the best-suited candidates. Add to this, the *General Questions* provide a strong indicator of the type of job candidate who will make the first cut. Let's look at a breakdown:

- Five of the 10 questions relate to **leadership** and working in a **team environment.**
- Two questions relate to **personal achievements** including your **entrepreneurial efforts.**
- Two questions relate to **job and/or intern experience.**
- One question relates to your **highest level of education.**

General Question 1

Have you ever been the president/ leader/ director of a group (can be a group in school, work, social activities, church etc.)?

If you click *yes*, you're asked to indicate the size of groups you've led from a choice of four ranges: 10 or fewer members; 11-25 members; 26-50 members; more than 50 members.

Intriguing, isn't it? No matter what job your apply for, the very first question Google asks you is whether or not you've held a leadership position.

Google seeks fearless leaders.

What are the qualities of a leader? A person of high intelligence with a capacity for forward thinking. Someone who can successfully communicate with team members while inspiring them to do their best work. In short, a leader gets things done by managing the team synergy of individuals at every juncture.

If you haven't led a team of geeks in the development of amazing code, don't panic. Your leadership experience doesn't have to be headline-worthy to catch Google's attention. Have you ever led a group of hikers on a nature walk? Or, directed a volunteer neighborhood clean-up? Did you ever lead club activities? These types of experiences qualify as a *yes*.

However, be prepared for a phone interviewer to probe your survey responses more deeply. For example, if you indicated you were president of your travel club, you may be asked to describe a time when you resolved conflict among members. Or, how you dealt with members who disagreed with you and challenged your authority. The possibilities are endless. The important thing is to clearly communicate in a way that illustrates your positive leadership qualities and grace under fire.

General Question 2

Compared to other people in your peer group, how would you describe the age at which you first got into (i.e., got excited about them, started using them, etc.,) computers on scale from 1 to 10?

The scale ranges from "Much later than others (I just learned to use the computer to fill out this résumé)," to "Much earlier than others (I was the first person in my peer group to use computers)."

Why include this question in the non-technical section of the survey? When you work for the *Masters Of The Online Universe,* you're expected to have a passion for technology no matter what your job title may be.

Google provides their people with the very latest technological tools, programs and intra-company communications. Basic computer skills will not suffice. And if you mention on your résumé knowledge of standard programs like MSWord, it's not going to impress them. This survey question also appears to be probing for deeper bio-data.

Google seeks candidates who have traits in common with founders.

Let's follow the clues:

- Larry Page reports having a passion for computers since age six
- Sergey Brin got his first computer at age nine
- Both of the Google Founders attended Montessori schools as children
- Together, they leveraged a graduate school dissertation into an amazing global company

If you can communicate your similarities to Google's founders, could it increase your chances at landing the job? Of course it could. We're talking about traits which contributed to the development of a company – a passion for technology, innovative critical thinking and some risk taking.

General Questions 3, 5 and 10

What is your ideal project team size (number of team members)?

Please indicate your working style on a scale of 1 (Work alone) to 5 (Work in a team).

When you think about your past experiences with working in teams, would you say you typically worked ... in teams of more than 40 members; in teams with 21 to 40 members; in teams with 10 to 20 members; in teams with fewer than 10 members; you have never worked in a team before.

With three questions dedicated to teamwork experience, it's obvious you need to exhibit the capacity to work in Google's unique team-oriented environment.

Prepare in advance for interview questions about your teamwork skills.

Work up a list of every team-oriented experience you've ever had – in school, at work (don't overlook part-time jobs), plus church and civic projects. Then ask yourself a few questions:

- How did your work and unique talents benefit the team?
- How well did you handle your assigned tasks?
- What did you like about working in a team?
- Can you recount an occasion when you stepped up to solve a problem?

Once you jog your memory, you'll see you have more applicable team experience than you realize. Answer the survey's teamwork questions with confidence and keep these notes in a Google doc so they are handy for your first phone interview.

General Question 6

Please indicate all the languages you speak and your level of proficiency in each. (Choices include: very basic knowledge; conversational; somewhat fluent; fluent.)

This seems a logical query from a global company with customers worldwide. Except for the fact the survey allots seven slots for your response. How many Google applicants speak seven different languages? We have no idea. But we suspect Google may be mining for deeper bio-data. Research indicates learning multiple languages boosts your brain power in the area which processes information. Add to this, the younger you are when learning multiple languages, the more robust your thinking process will be. Could this be Google's underlying reason for inquiring about your multi-lingual talents? We believe it is.

No matter how basic your knowledge of a foreign language, include it on your survey response.

General Question 8

Have you ever turned a profit at your own non-tech side business (dog walker, catering, tutoring, etc.) ?
... started your own non-profit?

... started a club or recreational group?
... set a regional-, state-, country-, or world-record?

While the US Army promises to help you "be all you can be," it appears Google wants you to "be all that" before they give you a desk.

The core of question eight is probing your ability to take initiative and create something from the bottom up. As for record-setting, it's an attempt to see if you're willing to push the boundaries of your own abilities to reach a goal. Also pay attention to their interest in your non-profit work. They're looking for indicators of your willingness to collaborate for the good of the "team" without expectation of personal glory.

If you can communicate you in fact possess these traits at every stage of the Google recruitment process – the survey, your résumé, the phone interviews – you'll have an edge over candidates who fail to exhibit these traits.

Present your accomplishments in a way that satisfies Google's desired behavioral indicators.

General Questions 4, 7 and 9

How many years of related work experience do you have? (You should not count years of internship experience or classes in school.)
Were you ever a contractor, temporary worker, or intern at Google?
What is your highest level of education?

We thought it odd to find these questions on the survey considering they're usually standard on job applications. But when we checked out the <u>Google Job Application</u> it proved to be quite sparse. This begs the question: is the Google Job Survey the primary applicant filter? Of course it is.

In press piece after press piece, Google assures a real live person reviews each of the million-plus résumés they receive each year. Can this be humanly possible? Possibly. But one thing is obvious: the auto-scanned job surveys likely determine which applicants are interviewed first.

Let's face it, it's entirely possible Google can be in the midst of considering 1000-plus job candidates for the same job you're targeting. And every one of them possesses skills and experience on par with yours. To differentiate yourself from the other 999 candidates you must keep one thing in mind:

Landing a job at Google is more than joining a company, you're joining a movement built around a noble cause.

Convince them their cause is truly your own and your competitors will pale in comparison.

How To Use The Job Survey Questions to Prepare For Your Phone Interview

• Make a record of your responses to survey questions. We suggest using Google docs.

• Develop detailed "notes to self" expanding on your responses should the interviewer ask about your responses.

• Don't bluff. Don't add fluff. Any hint of exaggeration, inaccuracy (or lies) on your survey, résumé, or during interviews, will result in an automatic pass.

THE VOLUNTARY GOOGLE JOB SURVEY PART 2 – OVERVIEW

Whether you've been in the workforce several years or a recent grad, you'd better pull out your transcripts. On part two of the survey Google requests:

• SAT Math Score (range 200-800)
• SAT Critical Reading (formerly Verbal) Score (range 200-800)
• SAT Writing (section added after March 2005) Score (range 200-800)
• GRE Analytical Score (range 200-800)
• GRE Quantitative Score (range 200-800)
• GRE Verbal Score (range 200-800)

- Undergrad GPA (on a 4.0 scale)
- Graduate GPA (on a 4.0 scale)

Don't panic. Google recruiters know your GPA offers a partial picture of what you can bring to the table. That's why your responses to behavioral questions (on the survey and during interviews) are scrutinized.

After you complete the *10 General Questions*, the second part of the survey mines for deeper bio-data related to your selected job. You're asked to choose one of four broad categories:

- Advertising/Sales
- Engineering
- Staffing/HR
- Finance
- Other (there is no secondary survey for this category)

We've included a general overview of the secondary surveys to give you an idea of additional behavioral questions specific to each job discipline.

Low GPA? Spotty Work History?

Turn A Negative Into A Positive!

How can you turn a low GPA or spotty work history into positive? Explain what happened!

If your GPA suffered due to a family crisis or working two jobs to pay for school, tell them. If you've quit a job because you were searching to find your passion, tell them. Some people are unable to stay at a job because their skills were underutilized which resulted in boredom. And if you left a position to start your own business – even if the business failed – this would still be a positive for Google. Whatever your reason, tell them. Seriously, being accurate and honest with your personal experience is always the best strategy.

The Engineering Job Survey

A broad overview of question topics includes:

- What types of technology are you familiar with?
- Are you willing to be interviewed on the code languages you've selected?
- Have you worked or interned at other tech companies? (They list 15 of the majors.)

- Have you entered coding competitions and how well did you place?
- Were you ever a research assistant or a mentor?
- Did you ever publish an article or file a patent?
- Do you prefer developing theory or getting things done (on a scale from 1-5).

And, if this wasn't enough data to collect, other questions probe your personality type (forgiving, considerate and helpful vs. argumentative, critical and aloof) and working style (careless, lazy, efficient, and reliable). These are data points that assist Google in the decision making process. There is no right or wrong.

Overall, the Engineering Job Survey points to crucial areas of experience you should include on your résumé and discuss during interviews. But don't attempt to bluff your programming abilities. Software engineering is the lifeblood of Google and your hands-on coding skills will be tested during the screening process.

The Advertising/Sales Job Survey

A much shorter survey, it focuses on questions related to your management style, communication skills, and behavioral profile. However, unlike the engineering personality questions, people interested in advertising and sales jobs are screened for different traits:

- Outgoing, assertive and talkative
- Quiet, shy and inhibited
- Artistic interests
- Sophistication in art, music and literature

- Imaginative and enthusiastic
- Curious and inventive

It's clear Google is seeking Advertising/Sales candidates with a certain level of sophistication. Assertiveness is a positive however an aggressive sales style or *hard sell* approach is simply not Google-y. This is not something you can manipulate, simply answer accurately.

The Staffing/HR Job Survey

With 1-million-plus résumés to process per year, it's no surprise Google is always looking for top-notch staffing specialists. Add to this, all Google employees have recruitment responsibilities as part of their job description. That's right – you can look forward to being interviewed and evaluated by Googlers from a cross-section of departments. That's why you can't assume your interviewer has a Staffing/HR background similar to your own. This is important because they may not be as well practiced at interviewing as you.

The Staffing/HR Survey inquires about your experience recruiting for: Microsoft, eBay, Sun, Amazon, Yahoo, Apple, Oracle, Pixar, SGI, Adobe, McKinsey, IBM, Bain, Trilogy, and BCG. If you've worked for any of these companies, even on a short-term contract basis, include them on your résumé. Other survey questions explore your leadership skills and career path choices. Have you presented on a panel at an academic or industry conference? Are you currently working in the same field in which you received your undergraduate/graduate degree? If you were a part of a new product team, would you prefer to design the plan or carry out the plan? Remember, for every *yes* you indicate on the survey, be prepared for the topic to come up during your phone screen. Write out your experiences and keep your notes handy; you'll feel more confident when discussing it during the phone interview.

The Finance Job Survey

When analyzing the Finance Job Survey, we noticed Google includes the same behavioral questions asked of software engineers: do you see yourself as someone who is forgiving; considerate; helpful; kind (verses) argumentative; critical; rude and aloof?

Yes, it's the teamwork thing again. If you look at Google's *Finance Operations* job descriptions, you'll find verbiage such as:

• responsible for collaborating with finance, product management, and engineering....

• in conjunction with your colleagues....

• collaborate with internal and external stakeholders....

• responsible for collaborating with sales, product management and engineering....

• work directly with our talented software engineers as well as other key finance teams....

Your ability to communicate with, and summarize issues for, specialists beyond the realm of finance is crucial. Keep this in mind when you complete the general survey questions and the secondary questions.

Keep your answers accurate. Always assume the auto-scanner is searching for indicators specific to the job description to which you're applying.

Voluntary Job Survey Do's & Don'ts.

DO complete the survey, it give you an advantage over those who skip it.

DO give careful consideration to behavioral questions. Meaning accurate responses regarding your experience.

DO keep notes on your survey responses to prepare for the phone interviews. We recommend Google docs.

DO consider your high school accomplishments when responding to leadership questions.

DO NOT attempt to bluff about your work experience.

DO NOT exaggerate your programming/coding abilities; you will be tested.

DO NOT lie. Period. It may prevent you from being considered for future positions.

IS YOUR RÉSUMÉ/CV GOOGLE-Y?

You may be surprised to know Google has rejected MIT graduates and tech industry professionals from top-notch companies. Don't assume your CV pedigree is enough to impress them. It's crucial to *Google-fy* your résumé accomplishments to help boost your bio-data quotient.

Of course, all candidates fall into two major categories: recent graduates and professionals with work experience. However, the goal is the same for everyone – to brand yourself in a way that screams "*Google-y!*"

There's a wealth of information in the Joining Google section of the company website in addition to a separate section for Student Opportunities. Rather than simply reproduce the information here, we've "read between the lines" to guide you in presenting yourself as an achiever who meets Google's needs. Keep in mind, Google highly values:

- Intelligent, forward-thinking people intrigued by ideas and inspired by challenges.
- Interesting people with cool hobbies, talents, passions and skills.
- Fearless leaders who "step up to the plate," take the initiative and learn from mistakes.
- People with savvy interpersonal skills and *emotional intelligence.*
- Productive, entrepreneurial, results-oriented people with a clear vision they can communicate to others.

- Individuals who are willing to share knowledge, volunteer and collaborate because they understand "it takes a village."

Remember – the moment you submit your online application, résumé and completed job survey, your Google dossier is born. When you *Google-fy* your résumé, it adds positive data-points to your profile.

The Google Résumé Litmus Test.

Make sure …

… you can verify every accomplishment and college project on your résumé.

… you can clearly communicate relevant details about your accomplishments when asked during your phone interview.

… you can provide supporting documents if requested.

… you don't spam Google with multiple résumé submissions for a slew of open positions.

Your Résumé/CV – It's All About Your Achievements

We've all heard the tried-and-true résumé advice: look at the potential employer's job description and employ similar phraseology on your résumé/CV. Although it's a good idea to analyze the requirements of the position for which you're replying, we're talking about Google, here. If you simply mimic their recruitment terms, they're certain to notice. Instead, study the job description to ascertain the best way to present your achievements as they relate to the job requirements.

We looked at a cross-section of Google job listings—from software engineer jobs to marketing and customer service – and the same consistent phrases would arise:

Deep knowledge in ...

Deep experience in ...

Deep understanding of ...

A solid foundation in ...

A proven track record ...

Ability to work cross-functionally ...

Demonstrated ability to ...

No matter what Google position interests you, consider what Google is interested in knowing about you – are you a heavyweight in your area of expertise? How can you communicate such awesomeness in a résumé? Whether you're a working professional or a recent graduate, use the "Show, Don't Tell" approach when crafting your CV.

Don't tell them you have "a solid foundation in computer science," show them by discussing an application program you've written. Did you lead coding projects at college? Or, better yet, in your own free time?

You wouldn't program on your free time unless you loved it. NOW you're talking!

Rather than telling them you have, "Deep experience in sales team management," show specifics like, "Currently manage a sales team of 15 and increased sales by 5% in 4th quarter of 2010 by automating replenishment."

Don't tell them you have "a demonstrated ability to utilize web-based marketing programs," show them by naming the programs you've successfully utilized and support it with a concrete example like, "Increased web traffic by 30%." Were you innovative? Tell them.

At times, this may be difficult for those who feel uncomfortable boasting about their accomplishments. It's NOT boasting. It's an accurate detailing of your skills and qualifications. It might help to talk about your career milestones with a friend at university or a trusted colleague at work. Such discussions may also highlight other accomplishments they recall and you may have taken for granted.

When you look at the Joining Google website, you'll find the company is very specific about what they want to see on your résumé:

- Provide your job title, employer name and dates of employment.

- Provide a brief description of the companies you have worked for especially if they are not well known.

- Provide your specific "key accomplishments" in each role.

- We want to see concise (i.e. bulleted), important details on your key accomplishments and the impact your efforts had on your company. For engineering résumés, please include the programming languages and tools used for each.

- If you worked while attending a college/university, either during the summer or concurrent with your course work, be sure to mention this even if it isn't specifically related to a potential job at Google.

- Customize your résumé by highlighting the skills that are relevant to the position.

Remember – if you submit a generic résumé to Google it will end up in your dossier forever. This may cause you to lose the opportunity for which you've currently applied while negatively impacting your chances of getting a call when similar positions open in the future.

Google's favorite words in job requirements.

We have gone through hundreds of Google job requirements to identify the most common words. We then grouped these words by job categories and displayed them is tag clouds. The bigger the word, the most often it appears.

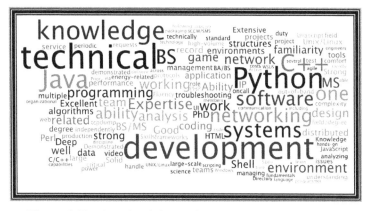

Figure 1: Engineering job requirement tag cloud

Figure 2: Finance job requirement tag cloud

Figure 3: Human Resources job requirement tag cloud

Figure 4: Marketing and Sales job requirement tag cloud

Google-Friendly Projects

It makes sense for recent grads to list college projects related to the job they want to land. But how about young professionals? A successful college project, especially one in which you held a leadership role, can indicate positive bio-data not well-reflected in your employment history. No matter what year you graduated college, if an achievement directly relates to the Google job you're targeting, consider adding to your résumé.

For example, if you're applying for a Google marketing position but currently work in a junior capacity with little opportunity to spearhead projects, think about your undergrad and graduate school accomplishments. Then, set up a résumé subheading for *Applicable College Experience* and list the *"Get Out To Vote"* campaign you piloted in college. Or, if you're currently working at a job unrelated to your degree in finance (thanks to a poor job market), list finance-related projects you completed when in college.

How about job candidates with a liberal arts background? The good news – you're in the running. In fact, there is a new trend for top companies to hire liberal arts majors. The not-so-good-news – you must craft your résumé in a way that proves you're not *just* an academic. Remember – Google seeks on-the-front-line entrepreneurial types with a track record for taking initiative. Here are examples of other Google-y college experiences to consider adding to your résumé/CV:

- Web-based business you launched when in college (mention if it turned a profit)
- Tutoring service you started in college (mention if it turned a profit)
- Green projects you launched and/or promoted (Google is super-Green)
- Overseas study projects (clearly identify how it relates to the job you seek)
- Research projects (add the professor's name, nature of your work, your role, etc.)

- Volunteer work (political campaigns, Habitat for Humanity, PETA, etc.)
- ANY college project in which GOOGLE PRODUCTS played a major role.

For those still a year or more away from graduation, start acquiring Google-desired accomplishments right NOW. Volunteer your skills to head a marketing project for a start-up business or non-profit you support. Start a small business utilizing your skills and work it from your dorm room. Web-based? Even better. Write a new app, just for fun! You could also volunteer your skills at a non-profit or start a non-profit of your own.

Awards, Published Articles & Off-The-Job Accomplishments

If you won first place in a Betty Crocker® cookie recipe contest, bravo! But don't list it in the awards section of your CV; list it under hobbies. If your article, "How To Perform CPR On Your 8-Week-Old Kitten," was published in <u>Cat Fancy Magazine</u>, we're impressed. And Google may be impressed, too. But this also belongs in the hobbies section.

Only list awards, published articles and professional accomplishments which show Google you have the right stuff. Examples:

- Entrepreneurial efforts like an online business you work from home in your spare time.
- Industry awards and published articles related to your selected job.

- Industry panels you've led which relate to your selected job.
- Open source coding , coding contests and developer challenges (especially Google's Developer Challenges).
- Mobile Apps you've created and shared – just for the fun of it.
- Personal interest websites and blogs – provide links and if you've used Google AdSense on your website, mention it!

Google-y Hobbies & Sports

Although a percentage of employers likely couldn't care less what you do in your spare time, Google does. Your hobbies and personal interests reflect major behavioral indicators. Make sure everything you list communicates you're an intriguing person with strong ideals, creativity and a good dose of optimism.

Look at it from Google's point of view. Let's say you're competing for a position with a candidate who's professional and college accomplishments are virtually identical to your own. Although your résumé does not include off-the-job interests, his/her résumé mentions:

- Studied art in Paris for two years.
- Took first place in cross-country skiing competition, 2005.
- Volunteered for the Gulf Shore clean-up after the BP oil spill, 2010.

Which of you would they be more interested in interviewing? The other applicant shows they like to challenge themselves; are goal-oriented; know how to overcome adversity; and when they are passionate about an issue, they DO something about it. Wouldn't you want to hire someone who could bring those qualities to your company?

Philosophy Alert!

While crafting your résumé/CV, take a look at Google's Company Philosophy, "Ten things we know to be true." If any of your experiences and/or projects align with these core principals, include them on your résumé.

More About The Recent Grad's Résumé

How can you craft a Google-y CV when you haven't yet worked in a related industry? Again, it's all about your accomplishments. In fact, recent grads may actually have more latitude in what they can include on their résumé.

No matter what school you attended, your GPA carries weight at Google. However, if you took a year off to travel, or worked at your local computer repair shop to earn money for tuition, this could not only offset a less-than-stellar GPA, it will indicate you've got good old fashioned gumption. Go ahead and list part-time jobs, summer jobs, or if you work at the family business. But be certain to clarify your role and specific accomplishments while on the job.

Include all research teams you were involved with, highlight your specific role and how you brought value to the project. Don't forget to note important projects you've completed for courses related to the position you seek.   If you worked as a research assistant, list the professor's name and contact information. While you're at it, list two additional professors as references.

Did you launch an entrepreneurial enterprise while at school? List it as a part-time business, describe your concept, and mention its profitability. It wasn't profitable, do you know why? Tell them, not all businesses are profitable in the beginning. If you are able to learn the reasons why it wasn't profitable, you learned a valuable business lesson.   List links to personal blogs and websites but, before you hit submit on the Google job site, read the next section first.

Google-fy Your Online "Brand" (Presence)

Forgive us for stating the obvious: **Google will google you.** And your online "brand" will give them copious bio-data about you. Always strive to make certain your Internet persona reflects how you want to be seen by Google and other potential employers.

You don't want recruiters to find that photo of you barfing behind the beer kiosk at the Oktoberfest. And you don't want them to read your *tweets* about the experience, either. And remember the YouTube video of the fist-fight you had with your roommate? You really don't want them to see that one.

Sanitize your online footprint

A 2010 Microsoft study indicates 70% of HR managers and recruiters in the US, Canada, and in Europe, rejected job candidates due to their negative online antics. Yet, fewer than 15% of applicants believed a negative presence would cause them to lose a job opportunity.

Don't be one of the uninformed. Before you list links to your website, blog or Facebook page, scrub any non-Google-y content. What types of content need to be considered?

BAD: An arrogant, mean-spirited rant that demeans others. Delete it. GOOD: An intelligent rant, with well-supported arguments, that shows you have positive, constructive passions. Keep it. You get the idea.

Ask yourself this: Does your online persona accurately describe you?

Remember, a positive online footprint can work to your favor during the Google recruitment process.

- Create good, informative blog and website content which showcases not only your IQ but also your emotional intelligence.
- Add a portfolio to your personal website which includes professional and college projects you've completed.
- Update and complete your LinkedIn profile, your Google profile, and the professional section of your Facebook page.
- Participate in forums and message boards related to your desired Google position; make sure your comments are of value and the information you share is pertinent.
- Cross-link all of the above on your website's home page and include links to your published articles.

Your Google Dossier Part 2 – Consider The Big Picture

Assume every bit of your bio-data will end up in your Google dossier in one form or another. From your job survey responses and résumé, to your online activity and interactions with interviewers, each component will paint your "big picture" in the minds of the hiring committee.

Will content from your personal website be added to your dossier? There's no confirmation of this, currently. However, our research shows many Google interviewers search online to see what they can find out about you. As a result, your personal website and blog will provide them with a "first impression" before your first phone interview. If your online persona presents poorly, it will subconsciously affect the interviewer and impact the ratings they enter in your dossier.

We know it's easy to apply online for a Google position. Perhaps it's too easy. Before you click *submit*, take the time and effort to carefully consider the information you're providing to Google. You don't want to receive the dreaded, "not at this time" email.

Résumé Basics Preferred By Google

- PDF or MS Word files are preferred (text formats are also acceptable).

- Put your name and contact information on all submitted documents (i.e. résumé, cover letter, portfolio samples, college transcripts)

- Include the full name of all post-secondary institutions, degrees conferred, and a cumulative grade point average for each degree.

- Only your college/university-level education needs to be reported on your résumé/CV.

- If you completed a "year abroad" college program, include.

- Whenever you use an acronym <u>also</u> spell it out (example: MBA Masters In Business Administration).

- Use bullets wherever possible and SEO-rich terms.

- Include college projects you completed which relate to the position you seek.

- Make certain everything on your résumé can be verifiable – no fluff, no bluff.

THE GOOGLE PHONE INTERVIEW – SCREENING FOR FALSE POSITIVES

If your survey responses and résumé duly impress Google, they'll set up the first of up to three phone interviews (each runs approximately 30 minutes). Make no mistake about it, these sessions are designed to rule you out as a candidate. They're not looking for reasons to hire you. They're looking for signs your bio-data may have registered a *false positive*.

In the first phone screen, a Google recruiter has two goals: to confirm the basic skills you've claimed on your résumé and to ascertain if you're a good fit for the Google culture. After analyzing hundreds of post-interview testimonials online, it appears many aspiring candidates were not prepared for the most basic questions. Even more amazing, Google lays out these basics for every applicant and gives fair warning on their website:

- Know what interests you about Google and why you've applied.
- Familiarize yourself with Google's products and services. Research our competitors.

- If you are interviewing for a software engineering or technical role, be ready to answer high-level technical questions on data-structures and algorithms. We would like you to code up your answers on boards with our engineers.

- Familiarize yourself with the job description you are interested in.

- If you are interviewing for a software engineering role then you may first want to visit the website www.topcoder.com. Please launch the "Arena" widget and go to the practice rooms where you can solve problems in the first and second division.

- Ensure you can substantiate anything your CV/résumé says – for instance, if you list Java or Python as your key programming language, questions about this are fair game and may be asked of you.

Why do you want to work for Google?

Every candidate is asked this question. And you may be asked this question by several interviewers. In fact, this may be the only question for which you can fully prepare in advance. Give it serious thought. Do a bit of soul searching. Why Google?

Yes, it's been described as the *Disneyland®* of employers. With its lava lamps, pool tables, mediation chairs and amazing free perks, it may be easy to forget Googlers work their hearts out. In fact, many in the tech industry believe Google's free on-site perks – haircuts, dental exams, childcare, gourmet-quality meals – are a way to keep employees at work for as many as 80 hours per week.

On his website, The Next Big Thing, Google Developer Advocate, Don Dodge, offers an inside look at what you can expect if hired:

"Google sets impossible bodacious goals…and then achieves them. The engineering mindset of solving the impossible problem is part of the culture instilled in every group at Google. Tough

engineering problems don't have obvious answers. You need to invent the solution, not just optimize something that exists."

When you're asked, *"Why Google?"* pre-canned responses found in books like <u>*Interviews For Dummies*</u> or <u>*How To Ace An Interview*</u> will simply not fly. Remember, your interviewer will be a staff Googler who works in the trenches every day. They were once in your shoes. They know how they had responded to this question. They know when you're slacking.

"Because it's a great company." Or, *"Because it's a place I can learn and grow,"* are woefully generic responses. Such responses are sure to trigger copious eye-rolling on the other end of the phone. The best type of response will exemplify your Google-y behavioral traits and provide evidence you've done your homework. Examples:

"Because everything I've read indicates Google is working on amazing new products this year. I want to be on the front lines of marketing ground-breaking technology like Google Voice. I want to utilize my proven marketing skills to make Google Voice a successful product "

"Because my research shows Google is looking for people who can develop awesome Mobile Apps. And this is something I'm passionate about. Let me show you… "

Put yourself in the interviewers' shoes. Who would make a better impression on you? The candidate who responds, "Because Google is a great place to work," or someone who delivers a meaningful, sincere, personal response?

"What do you know about Google products?"

s another question frequently asked by Google ters. It seems like a no-brainer. Surely everyone who interviews can speak intelligently about Android, AdWords, Google Earth, Chrome, and other Google innovations, right? Wrong.

Many interviewees fumble the *product* questions. In fact, a new graduate vying for a marketing position reported she'd managed to get all the way to the on-site interview – an amazing feat in itself – only to come up empty when asked about Google AdWords. She didn't get the job. Before you chuckle at her massive mistake, ask yourself if you're fully prepped to talk about Google products. Don't assume you know enough to wing it. Do your homework.

Start with Google's link to products and services. Take the initiative to study and use as many as you can (many are free). For AdWords, Google's Beginner's Guide is loaded with information. Also consider opening an AdWords account to further familiarize yourself. If you're applying for a position in marketing or product management, knowledge of AdWords is crucial. You may be quizzed via an online AdWords worksheet and you will be timed.

"What sort algorithm has the best worst-case runtime?"

If you're a software engineer, you'll be fielding a battery of technical questions. For you, the first phone interview is all about eliminating lesser-skilled engineers. Although Google is renowned for asking engineering applicants to code on demand, recruiters report a growing percentage fail at even basic coding challenges. Don't be one of them.

You'll be tested on program languages you've listed on your résumé and job survey. Be prepared to open a shared Google Doc and work problems to prove your proficiency. If you can't write a loop that goes from 1 to 10 in all languages you've claimed to know, you will not move to the next stage of the hiring process. The interviewer will end the session and send you a nice rejection email. Unfortunately, your lack of performance will be entered in your Google dossier. Should you reapply in the future, this may resurface.

When it comes to your résumé, it's tempting to include every technology language in which you've had *some* experience. But if your skills are rusty in two or three (or six), it may be better to leave those out.

When Google says, "… be ready to answer high-level technical questions on data-structures and algorithms," they truly mean it. Include on your résumé only those in which you're certain you can perform well. For a deeper look at Google's criteria for screening software engineers, check out the book "Cracking the Coding Interview" or "Programming Interviews Exposed".

"And now I will ask you a nebulous question."

Many interviewees (in various disciplines) report frustration when Google interviewers ask unspecified or nebulous questions. Don't be tempted to stumble your way through an answer rather than admit you need more information. Google interviewers may be vague with intention. They want to know if you can ask intelligent questions to better define parameters before you attempt a response. The ability to ask pertinent, intelligent questions is essential to teamwork and shows your critical thinking skills. Don't miss an interview opportunity to prove you can ask excellent questions.

Overview of Question Topics

No single resource can provide you with the exact questions recruiters will pose. With Google staffers conducting your interview – smart, savvy individuals who have made the grade – there's no telling what they'll decide to throw at you.

Setting aside software engineers (whose coding knowledge is vigorously tested), attempting to memorize answers to specific "Google Interview Questions" you find online may work against you.

If your interviewer doesn't ask questions you've anticipated, it may throw you off your game. Even worse, you may fumble the questions they do ask. Worse yet, if they ask a question you've researched, your pre-canned answer may reflect badly on you.

It's far better to familiarize yourself with the topic areas consistently covered in the Google interview process. These include:

The Company, Its Products & Its Competition.

- The reasons you want to work for Google.
- Your familiarity with Google products and services.
- Features you would like to see added to specific products and/or services. This is the kind of

innovative thinking /input they want from employees.

- Ways in which you would improve specific Google products and services. Now, we're talking!
- Your knowledge of Google's top competitors, their products and how Google can best compete with them (especially Facebook).
- Whether or not you're current with the latest technology trends (join and participate in newsgroups).
- Your knowledge of Mobile Apps as they may apply to the position (an engineer may be asked if they've designed Apps; a marketing candidate may be asked how they'd advertise a new app).
- Your passion for technology and ability to work with new technology.

Behavioral Tendencies, Communication Skills & Google-y Traits.

- Creative and or analytical thought processes when asked to solve a hypothetical problem (think out loud – Googlers love when you explain your thinking process).
- Willingness to risk being wrong and rapidly learn from your mistakes.
- Your ability to take the initiative and go above and beyond when tackling an assignment.
- Leadership potential – past, present and future.
- Ability to explain complexities to people with little technical knowledge.
- Grace under fire; decision-making process when under pressure.

- Emotional intelligence and natural ability to play nice with others.

Résumé- & Job-Specific Questions

- Anything included on your résumé will be explored; prepare to provide deeper details, examples and answer any possible question based on the information you provided. This includes hobbies listed on your résumé.
- Any topic in the job description for which you've applied may be posed as a question; it's also helpful to study other Google job descriptions in other areas of expertise to anticipate questions testing your cross-functional skills.
- Job-specific, hypothetical scenarios may be posed in an effort to see how you would find a resolution.
- For software engineers, extensive coding questions, of course. (Check out papers published by Google engineers to familiarize yourself with the company's latest technology.)
- For non-tech positions, candidates may be asked to write essays describing how they would handle hypothetical job-related challenges and projects.
- As the saying goes: expect the unexpected.

Update On The Famous Google Puzzle Questions

The Internet is rife with rumors about Google's brain-busting riddle questions designed to test your mathematical skills, critical thinking skills, creative thinking skills and IQ. Some leave you feeling less than smart or confused!

"How many golf balls can fit in a school bus?" (This very question was asked in an interview in March 2011.)

"How much would you charge to wash all the windows in Seattle?"

"A man pushed his car to a hotel and lost his fortune. What happened?

According to current and former Google recruiters, such riddle questions were banned years ago. However, our research indicates tough logic questions and mathematical word problems are still fair game if they relate to the job you would do when hired.

For example, if you're interviewing for a product manager spot, you may be asked how you would estimate the total cups of coffee people in Manhattan drink per day. Are they asking you to provide a sum figure? Or, are they asking you to explain the method you would use to arrive at an estimate? It's clearly the latter. Don't worry about being right, impress them with your thought process and you'll be ahead of the game.

Ask A Friend To Pre-Interview You On The Phone.

A little role-playing couldn't hurt. Compile questions built around items listed on your résumé and ask a friend to play the interviewer role on the phone. It would also help if your friend used different interview styles: the impatient interviewer; the cheerful interviewer; the just-the-facts interviewer who cuts you off to avoid tangential discussions.

The point of the exercise is to discover your soft spots and work on them before your Google interview. For example, do you get nervous when asked personal questions? Are you hesitant to talk about your accomplishments because you're not one to brag? It's best to discover such speed bumps before your phone interview.

Experiment with the type of hands-free phone equipment you prefer. Keep in mind a speaker phone can possibly create an echo. This may distort your voice and distract the interviewer. A headset may be a better choice. Either way, it's a good idea to leave your hands free if you're asked to open a Google Doc and write an essay or solve a coding problem.

Exploit Opportunities To Demonstrate Your Google-y-ness

If you were a computer prodigy at age three, find a way to slip it into the interview. If, like the company founders, you attended a Montessori School, look for an opportunity to mention it. Find ways to subtly show your interviewer you possess all the preferred Google-y traits. If possible, work in a mention of something amazing you've recently accomplished. It doesn't hurt to surprise your interviewers with something not currently in your dossier.

Also look for opportunities to turn potential negatives into positives. For example, if you worked your way through school, this could explain a lower GPA while revealing behavioral positives: you work hard to achieve your goals. Or, perhaps you dropped out of school to start your own consultant business. Your entrepreneurial spirit will earn points that make up for your lack of an earned degree.

Back Door Referrals

Google places a high value on candidates referred by their staff. In fact, referred candidates are often given priority and moved to the front of the interview line. Considering Googlers can earn generous bonuses when one of their referrals is hired, they're motivated to recommend you.

You need to be bold and proactive. Get out there and make connections with Googlers. Impress them with your Google-y-ness and passion for technology. At over 24,000 employees and rapidly growing, Googlers shouldn't be hard to find.

- Attend industry talks where Googlers are listed as speakers; introduce yourself during the meet and greet.
- Join open coding projects and shine! This is almost a working interview!
- Look for online articles written by Googlers, send an email discussing your views on the topic, and initiate a dialogue.
- Participate on message boards where Googlers discuss Google products.
- Network with Googlers on LinkedIn via the groups you belong to in LinkedIn. LinkedIn etiquette: Do not ask to be connected if you do not know the person. Do not ask to be introduced by someone

you barely know. Do read the Googler's postings and make thoughtful, meaningful comments.

- Contact school alumni who now work at Google.
- Only send friend requests to Googlers on Facebook after you have initiated dialogue in other forums, blogs or message boards. An out of the blue friend request is probably not welcome.
- Ask your family, friends, and friends of friends if they know Googlers.
- Research your university alumni as well.

When people share the same passions, it's easy to strike up conversations and make solid connections. An added bonus – when you network with Googlers you gain deeper insight into what the company looks for in a job candidate.

Low-Tech Ways To Prep For Your Phone Interview.

Relax! Meditate, go for a run, take a sea salt bath – do whatever it takes to put you in a calm state of mind before your phone rings at the appointed time. Nothing rattles interviewers more than a candidate who sounds like he or she is about to have an emotional breakdown.

Dress For Success. Yes, we know it's a phone interview. But you're more likely to bring your A-game when dressed business casual as opposed to lounging in your PJs. Freshly showered and wearing crisp clothing, you'll have that unflappable I-feel-good-about-myself attitude which resonates with interviewers.

Smile. Think about it – people who have a smile in their voice during phone conversations make for more pleasant interactions. With a smile in your voice, you may keep the interviewer on the line a bit longer gaining more time to prove your worth.

THE ON-SITE INTERVIEW

When you're invited for an on-site interview, you can rest assured Google already thinks you're exceptional. Less than one-percent of phone interviewees are invited to one of Google's global headquarters for a one-on-one. But don't make the mistake of feel *too special* or you may drop the ball in the final stretch. Keep your eyes on the prize! This is the time to focus.

The on-site interview is intense. Every interview question, written test and interaction is structured to assess ...

- if your soft skills/personality traits are a good fit for the (sometimes chaotic) Google culture.
- if your core competencies and work skills are exceptional.
- if your communication skills complement the team-oriented structure.
- if you can be productive and self-manage within a flat-organizational structure.
- if you'll be a true asset to the team you would join when hired.

The moment you enter the reception area, your interview begins. Be cordial, be communicative and, if the person at the reception desk appears stressed or grumpy, be nice. S/he may choose to mention your sunny attitude (or lack thereof) to the hiring committee.

In fact, a recent Harvard study indicates your likeability factor in the workplace may carry more weight than you may realize:

A recent Harvard Business School study looked at the effects of being likeable in the workplace. The results were interesting: Although we all obviously prefer to work for people who have both people skills and competence, when given a choice between one or the other, people overwhelmingly prefer a likeable person over a highly skilled person who is a poor communicator. New York Daily News, March 18, 2011.

You're In The Final Stretch

If you'd thought the phone screens were tough, you'd better get a solid night's rest before you head out for the on-site. It's a day-long encounter which can include up to six 45-minute one-on-one interviews, a panel interview, plus an interview over lunch.

Much like the phone interviews, you'll be fielding questions from a cross-section of Googlers. In fact, an one-on-one with your future manager is quite rare. As a result, people you may not work with *if hired* have a say in whether or not you *are hired*.

The reason – the Google flat management and collaborative culture. Some managers may not have much experience hiring and this keeps everyone on equal footing. Also, it keeps managers from hiring people with traits and backgrounds much like their own. When this happens, teams begin to lack diversity of thought and outlook. When Googlers from various departments conduct your interviews, it's easier to assess your ability to collaborate with a range of homogenous teams.

And the recruitment group-sourcing continues -- remember your Google dossier? Every current staff Googler also has a dossier on file. Google searches dossiers of their current employees to find matches who attended your school, or previously worked at your current company, during the same years listed on your résumé. These Googlers will receive an email asking for their opinion of you. And their feedback is entered into your dossier.

Although Google has been criticized for their consensus approach to employee recruitment, it can possibly work in your favor. Let's say you're vying for a finance-related position and one of your interviewers works in a support role. S/he is likely to focus on the quality of your communication skills versus your less-than-comprehensive knowledge of SQL.

Another advantage – when interviewed by Googlers who do not work directly with your (future) manager, they're more likely to offer unbiased views about the department you hope to join.

The Behavioral Thing ...again

Although you'll continue to be tested and evaluated by how your skills and qualifications match their needs, keep in mind your behavioral traits are always being observed. You may believe you're sitting alone, waiting for the next interviewer, but someone may be watching and surreptitiously taking notes.

For example, they may ask you to wait in a room where all sorts of fun gadgets are spread across the conference table. If they observe you sitting quietly, hands folded in your lap, it may be perceived as disinterest on your part. Even if you're dying to tinker, you may feel you're expected to sit politely. Don't make this mistake. Google prefers curious, inventive people who tinker with things and explore their surroundings.

There's a logical reason why Google uses such techniques when recruiting. Hiring the wrong candidate is not only costly, it can set back other teams and negatively impact vital projects or new-product launches.

The Interviewers

It warrants repeating – as with phone interviews, your on-site sessions will be conducted by Google employees from a range of departments and disciplines. Some may be well practiced at conducting interviews, while others, possibly recent hires themselves, may be less experienced. The onus in on you to impress them.

Don't ask your interviewers if you did well or if you've answered a question properly. They're restricted from sharing feedback with you. In fact, interviewers are restricted from sharing opinions of candidates amongst themselves. Every effort is made to gather the most accurate, unbiased "big picture" of you.

Now, let's take a moment to talk about another issue you may encounter: grumpy Google interviewers. Although the Internet is the perfect haven for anonymous griping, we did notice a large percentage of Google interviewees had at least one negative interaction with one of their on-site interviewers. Many candidates stressed the majority of their interviewers were "nice," however there was always one stand-out characterized as abrupt, irritable or arrogant.

Such moodiness is clearly not Google-y but there could be a couple of very logical explanations. If your interviewer is on deadline with a project, s/he may be anxious about taking time away from their work to conduct your interview. Or, equally as likely, you've been set up with a grumpy interviewer to test your performance under less-than-ideal circumstances.

Either way, no matter how nervous, frustrated, or jet-lagged you may be, never let them see you sweat. At Google, every employee's opinion counts. This includes their opinion of you.

ON-SITE ASSESSMENT TESTS

Non-Tech and support job candidates may be asked to take skill assessments, logic tests, grammar tests, and complete worksheets directly related to the position for which they've applied. Be prepared to write essays during the on-site interview. Questions and topics will relate to work skills required for your position should they hire you.

For example, an administrative assistant may be asked to plan an off-site special event within a specific budget for x-number of attendees. Or, a marketing writer may be expected to compose an email blast for a new Google product. Though written tests and essays are usually designed around situations you'd handle on the job, as a non-tech job candidate you may also be tested on your technological savvy or mathematical skills.

Software engineers will be required to work on complex code, logarithms and mathematical problems. Some work, including design, will be conducted on a whiteboard as Google engineers look on. Once again, you will be tested on languages in which you claimed proficiency. Veterans of the Google on-site interview recommend memorizing reference manuals in the event you're asked questions like: "What is the C-language command for opening a connection with a foreign host over the Internet?"

Recent Graduates: Common Interview Blunders

The good news: Google hires a number of new grads in the belief they can be more easily groomed to fit the Google culture. The bad news: Google's intense recruitment process is a minefield for recent grads who have little or no experience interviewing.

A 2011 CareerBuilder poll lists the top complaints of recruiters from major corporations, including Google recruiters. Listed here are those likely to be typical new grad blunders:

- 71% - Answering a cell phone or texting during the interview. (Turn your phone off.)
- 69% - Dressing inappropriately. (Google prefers **business** casual, not dorm casual.)
- 69% - Appearing disinterested. (Is there somewhere else you'd rather be?)
- 66% - Appearing arrogant . (Yes, we know you're very smart; that's why you're here.)
- 59% - Chewing gum. (Google provides you with healthy beverages, snacks and lunch; you won't starve.)

- 35% - Not providing specific answers. (Don't bluff, evade or fake it, ever. If you don't understand a question, ask for clarification.)

- 32% - Not asking good questions. (Asking about the pay rate **before** they make an offer is **not** a good question).

A new grad may also make the mistake of interacting with young Google interviewers (some being recent grads themselves) as if they were peers or confidants. Don't assume that young, hip Google interviewer is cool with your antics. At Google, employees who interview you are assessed on their interviewing skills. They will not risk their own jobs to cover for you.

If you've always dreamed of landing a Google job upon graduation, you might want to consider interviewing at other tech companies first. While other companies tell a candidate why they've been turned down, Google merely sends a "not a good fit" email. Lining up a few test runs can help you identify your weak spots before you attempt the Google interview gauntlet.

15 Google-y Traits Interviewers Look for In A Candidate.

- Significant and demonstrable leadership skills.

- Able to self-manage and self-motivate.

- A natural entrepreneurial spirit.

- Inspired by a team environment.

- Excellent communication skills.

- Adept at working with a cross-section of individuals.

- An ongoing, lifelong passion for computers.

- Able to transform ideas into products.

- A risk-taker in solving problems who can adapt to failures.

- Excited about taking on new challenges.

- The flexibility to adapt to rapid change.

- Able to thrive in a state of constant flux.

- A deep desire to learn and share knowledge.

- A *Green* concern for the environment.

Creative, smart, interesting and *"Google quirky."*

Your Interviewers Liked You.

Alas, you're not over the finish line. Next, your dossier is submitted to a **Hiring Committee** dedicated to the job classification for which you've been interviewed. At this point, a panel of senior managers, directors and employees review all of your documents; interview rating scores; written tests and essays; and all opinions/commentary tracked in your dossier. Keep in mind, although no member of the committee has met with you, arriving at a consensus opinion is the goal.

If your performance impresses the Hiring Committee, your dossier is forwarded for an **Executive Review** conducted by senior management and VPs. If they approve, your application is forwarded to the **Compensation Committee** which will determine your salary offer. However, before they present you with a formal offer, you must pass a **Final Executive Review** where one of Google's top executives makes a final determination. Only then will your recruiter present an offer package. Is it any wonder the entire recruitment process can take up to six months?

MAKE 2011 THE YEAR YOU GET HIRED AT GOOGLE

As we approach the launch date of this book, more exciting reports indicate a diversity of new positions opening at Google. Many of these are a result of Google's $700-million acquisition of ITA, a software company in Cambridge, Massachusetts.

ITA software provides flight schedules and pricing information for booking trips online. This software is used by most major airlines and leading online travel services such as Orbitz and Hotwire.com.

The decision, which allows Google to expand into the online travel market, comes as new CEO Larry Page revamped the company's management structure in a bid to accelerate efforts in social networking, mobile and other key businesses. ... The ITA buy is part of an acquisition and hiring spree as Google aims to ensure its online services stay on top as Internet surfers go mobile and turn to services like the wildly popular Facebook. Reuters.com, April 11, 2011.

So far this year, Google has acquired new office space in Venice and Beverly Hills, CA, to accommodate Google and Google-owned You Tube employees who will be developing quality content related to the entertainment industry. These announcements coincide with Larry Page recently taking over as CEO. He's clearly ramping up to move Google deeper into new arenas.

A recent article by Seth Weintraub in *Fortune Magazine* says it all in its title: It's Time To Stop Thinking About Google As A Search Company.

The notion that Google is 90+% search hasn't been true for a long time, but lately it's become obvious: YouTube, AdSense, Enterprise and location/mapping are becoming huge businesses in their own right and together may have replaced search as Google's biggest revenue generator. Fortune, March 29, 2011

Without a doubt, this year offers the best opportunity to date to land a Google job. Get started now. Use the tools and techniques we've provided then head over to Google and check out the Jobs section or Student Opportunities.

The Perks.

An overview of the amazing benefits and perks you'll enjoy when you get a job at Google. Of course keep in mind that the perks and benefits vary depending on the google office & country:

Superior Medical Benefits plus Comprehensive Dental & Vision Insurance

Free Employee Assistance Program

Comprehensive Life, Accident & Disability Insurance

401(k) & College Savings Plan

Vacation (15 days the first year), Maternity & Parental Leave Plus Perks for New Moms & Dads

Tuition Reimbursement

Employee Referral Plan

Back-Up Childcare

RESOURCES

Google: Corporations That Changed the World. Virginia Scott. Greenwood Publishing Group

Programming Interviews Exposed. John Mongan, Noah Suojanen and Eric Giguère. WROX

Cracking the Coding Interview. Gayle Laakmann McDowell

AdWords Beginner's Guide. Google

Everything Google (Google products), Google

Google's philosophy, Google

Google's history, Google

TopCoder Competition Arena. TopCoder

Programming Interview Questions, CareerCup

How Google sets goals and measures success. Don Dodge

It is time to stop thinking of Google as a Search company. CNN Money

Employers Reveal Outrageous and Common Mistakes Candidates Made in Job Interviews, careerbuilder.com

America's Ideal Employers 2011, Universum

With 3,000 job applications a day, Google can be picky. USA today

Google Answer to Filling Jobs Is an Algorithm, The New York Times

Google Co-Founder Larry Page Takes Over From CEO Eric Schmidt, Wired

A Gaggle Of Google Critics, The Washington Post